YOUR KNOWLEDGE HAS VALUE

AF125513

Nestle's Practices in the International Marketing Management

Ali Al Ghail

Bibliographic information published by the German National Library:

The German National Library lists this publication in the National Bibliography; detailed bibliographic data are available on the Internet at http://dnb.dnb.de.

ISBN: 9783346868732
This book is also available as an ebook.

© GRIN Publishing GmbH
Trappentreustraße 1
80339 München

Print and binding: Books on Demand GmbH, Norderstedt, Germany
Printed on acid-free paper from responsible sources.

The present work has been carefully prepared. Nevertheless, authors and publishers do not incur liability for the correctness of information, notes, links and advice as well as any printing errors.

GRIN web shop: https://www.grin.com/document/1355321

Report of Nestle Company Practices in International Marketing Management

International Marketing Management Analysis

Athena Global Education &
Guglielmo Marconi University

By

Ali Al Ghail
March 21, 2022

Table of Contents

List of Figures

List of Tables

Executive Summary

This report has evaluated and analyzed the international marketing management practices of Nestle Company. It has started with providing a clear picture of the company, such as its product portfolio, vision, mission, brands, values, and corporate business principles. It identifies the international marketing strategies that Nestle uses, which include the 7 Ps of marketing mix strategies and the STP marketing model.

The paper highlighted three issues the company faces in the international marketing environment. These include the political conditions and instability that create new laws, the economic conditions of the various countries, and the social and cultural factors, using Nestle India's Maggi Noodles event in 2015 as an example. It also showed that, it depended on the localization approach and an acquisition strategy to expand and enter new international markets. While the best international entry methods for the company are joint ventures, foreign direct investment, and wholly owned subsidiaries, applying the Porter Model and Ansoff Matrix together for selecting the international market entry and developing the strategy of entry successfully is also important.

Moreover, the report showed brand management through the CBBE model and applied it to the Cerelac brand category of Nestle Company. It also discussed how to develop the new brand strategy and apply it to the new Life Cuisine brand of the company. It also discussed the NDP process and its key strengths, which involve increasing the competitive advantage, quality, and value of the company, as well as its weaknesses, which include its complexity and risk, changes in the sourcing of ingredients, and shelf-life stability.

Furthermore, this study provided new international marketing strategy recommendations for expanding the business of Nestle in the international marketplace. After that, it devised an international marketing plan for launching a new food product at Nestle successfully. The plan showed how to implement the strategy from the first to the last step, involving timelines, key players, and actionable tasks.

Chapter 1: Introduction

1.1 The Nestle Company's Profile

Nestle SA is a Swiss multinational food product and beverage manufacturer that was founded in 1905 through the integration of the Farine Lactée Henri Nestlé company that was established in 1867 by Henri Nestlé and the Anglo-Swiss Milk Company that was founded in 1866 by two brothers, George and Charles Page. The company's headquarters are in Vevey, Vaud, Switzerland. Today, it is the largest food and beverage company in the world, with more than 2000 brands present in 191 countries and 376 factories in 85 countries around the world, with a total sale of 84,343 million CHF. It has about 273,000 employees. Nestle gained its strong global brand through the use of properly designed local and international marketing strategies (Nestlé, 2021). The main competitors include ConAgra Foods, Unilever, Kraft Foods Group, Hansen Natural Corporation, Mondelz International, and Monster Beverage Corporation (Reza, 2020).

Nestle's mission is *"Good Food, Good Life"* this statement refers to the company's belief in the power of food to enhance the lives of everyone through providing the best-quality beverages, foods, and nutritional health solutions. While the vision of the company is to be a leading, competitive Nutrition, Health, and Wellness company that delivers improved shareholder value by being a preferred employer, preferred corporate citizen, and preferred supplier while selling preferred products. The values of the company focus on the conception of honesty, fairness, and concern for individuals and families, communities, and the planet (Nestlé, 2021). The corporate business principles of the Nestle Company concentrate on six factors, as shown in Figure 1.

This figure was removed due to copyright reasons.

Figure 1: Nestle's Corporate Business Principles
Source: (Nestle, 2020)

1.2 The Nestle's Product Portfolio and Brands

Nestle is the largest international company with a broad product portfolio of the most needed foods and beverages for pet care. Under these brands, it has 2,000 titles and a large portfolio. The company's main products will be classified into seven top categories. These seven categories include fevers, prepared cooking aids, petCare, nutrition and health science, milk products and ice cream; water; and confectionery (Nestlé, 2021). The company offers them under various brands, as demonstrated in Figure 2.

This figure was removed due to copyright reasons.

Figure 2: The Nestle's Product Portfolio and Brands, Source: (Nestlé, 2021)

1.3 The Nestle Company's Size

To determine the size of the Nestle company, it should find out the following factors, according to its last annual report:

- The number of its product lines and the volume of its sales revenue by product segmentation are shown in Figure 3.

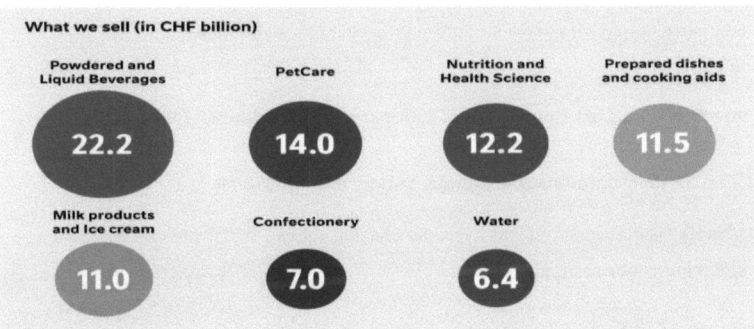

Figure 3: The Nestle's Sales Revenue by Product Segmentations in 2020

Source: (Nestlé, 2021)

- The number of markets in which the company operates in the world and its total sales in each geographical area are detailed in Figure 4. Europe, the Middle East, and North Africa (EMENA), the Americas (AMS), and Asia, Oceania, and sub-Saharan Africa (AOA).

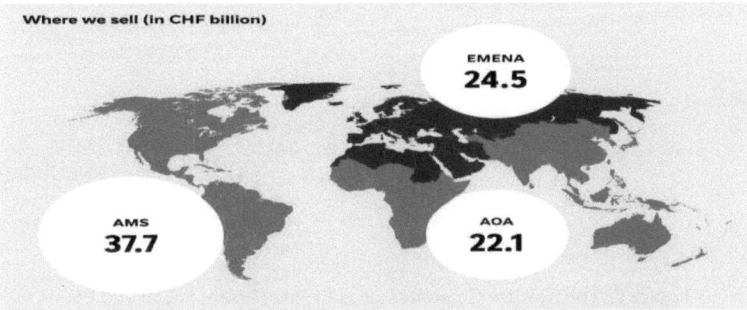

Figure 4: The Nestle's Sales by the Geographical Areas, Source: (Nestlé, 2021)

- The number of countries where the company sells its products, the employees' number, and the corporate taxes paid are detailed in Figure 5.

Number of employees	Number of countries we sell in
273 000	**186**
Total group salaries and social welfare expenses (in CHF)	Corporate taxes paid in 2020 (in CHF)
14 billion	**2.6** billion

Figure 5: Highlighted Data of Nestle Company in 2020, Source: (Nestlé, 2021)

1.4 The Nestle Commitment to People, Society and the Planet

To identify Nestle's commitment to people's health, society, and the planet in a clear picture, kindly look at Figure 6 below.

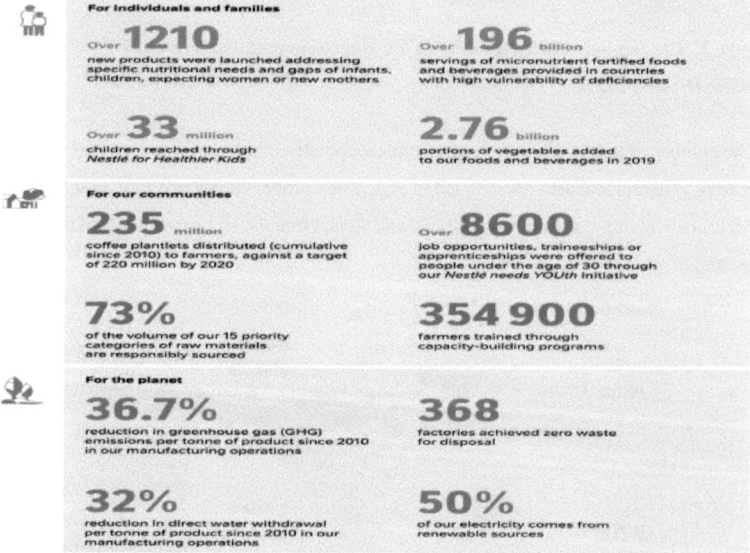

Figure 6: The Nestle's Commitment to People Health, Social and Planet

Source: (Nestlé, 2021)

1.5 The Performance of Nestle Company

Nestle relies on its health, nutrition, and wellness strategy to enhance its value creation. According to the 2020 annual report (Nestlé, 2021), compared to the previous year, the company has improved in profitability, organic sales growth, and capital efficiency, as illustrated in Figure 7.

Figure 7: The Highlighted Performance of Nestle Company in 2020
Source: (Nestlé, 2021)

1.6 Marketing Management Practices of Nestle Company

Local marketing refers to a company that has a limited geographic area for selling its products, while regional marketing refers to a company that has a large geographic area for selling its products and services, such as a district or group of smaller states. National marketing is when the company sells its products and services in a specific country (Topper, 2022). The global marketing approach indicates a company that holds its marketing operations at its main headquarters while selling its products or services globally in different countries. While international marketing refers to the company that can hold its marketing operations from its main subsidiary's offices that operate in different countries (Prachi, 2019).

Accordingly, it can be deduced that Nestle has a local and mostly international marketing strategy, as it operates its marketing activities not only from its main headquarters in Vevey, Vaud, Switzerland, but also from its factory offices around the world. The company has a long history of acquisitions and expansion of its markets worldwide that began with the 4Ps marketing mix strategies that contain product, price, place, and promotion. After that, Nestle S. A transfer to the extended 4Ps framework will consist of three added factors that include people, physical evidence, and process as part of the marketing mix (Reza, 2020), as will be identified in Table 1 below.

Nestlé's 7P's of MARKETIN MIX STRATEGIES	
Product	The company focuses on the most needed food and beverage products for nutrition, health, and wellness to enhance the lives of people, families, and pets and lead happier, healthier lives. These products include seven categories: powdered and liquid beverages; petCare, prepared dishes and cooking aids; nutrition and health science, milk products and ice cream; water; and confectionery (Nestlé, 2021).

Placing	Nestle sells its products through marketing channels that include supermarkets, an online website, hypermarkets, and wholesalers who then sell to different retailers (Addison, 2019).
Pricing	Lower price than other international brands and competitors with the best quality to maintain and enhance the loyalty of consumers (Reza, 2020).
Promotion	Nestle adopts a promotion mix by focusing on unique, extensive advertising and marketing its products and making customers aware of them. It uses a perfect blend of several different promotion tools such as TV, newspapers, social media, mass media, billboards, hoardings, e-mail, online ads, etc. (Singh et al., 2021).
People	Nestle has people who are trained in persuasive techniques and show respect to the business customer by focusing on their preferences. The team within the company is used to support the growth strategy of its products and achieve the marketing objective of the company through active performance (Addison, 2019).
Process	Nestle focuses on customer service to earn the loyalty of its customers by ensuring its products are always available at retail stores and using an online delivery process. It also works for researching market opportunities to understand customer needs (Addison, 2019).
Physical Evidence	Nestle uses the best packaging innovation, which covers a product with a distinct color and design to make it more attractive to consumers and easily identifiable on retail shelves. The company also has an online website that helps the customers see its products in high-quality images that have been taken from various angles (Addison, 2019).

Table 1: Nestlé's 7P's of Marketing Mix Strategies

Moreover, Nestle SA depends on the STP marketing model, which refers to segmentation, targeting, and positioning, to develop its specific and actionable international marketing strategies as detailed in Table 2.

The STP Marketing Model of Nestle Company		
Marketing Segmentation	**Targeting**	**Position**
Market segmentation helps the company to identify distinct consumer groups based on different characteristics and features. Nestle SA depends on four basic market segmentation-strategies (Reza, 2020): • Geographic • Demographic • Behavioral • Psychographic	The company uses targeting to select the groups with which it intends to engage. Nestle produces products according to different ages, lifestyles, seasons, and weather in Singapore, such as the Nescafe Ice products that contain cold caffeine for the customers in hot and warm weather (Singh et al., 2021).	The positioning of Nestle provides a vital role in international marketing by helping it to stand out among local and international competitors by creating unique products and brand images in clients' minds and improving their perception about the experience when they buy its products (Varma & Ravi, 2017).

Table 2: The STP Marketing Model of Nestle Co.
Source: (Hanlon, 2022)

Chapter 2: Literature Review

2.1 The Current Issues that Impact on the International Marketing Environment of Nestle Company

The definition of international marketing is simply the marketing of products and services in more than one country, like Nestle. All marketing activities face many challenges and issues due to the complexity and changing environment, whether due to internal or external factors. The internal factories impact the marketing of the company through its strategy and decisions that relate to implementing its mission, objectives, and values. The marketing environment can also affect the structure of the company, the characteristics of human resources, the internal power relationship, etc. (Yadav, 2009). Therefore, these forces can decrease the ability of the company to maintain its competitiveness and serve its customers, such as consumers, suppliers, and the public. While the external environmental factors can also have deep impacts on the marketing environment. These factors include political, economic, social, technological, environmental, and legal factors (PESTLE) (Agwu & Onwuegbuzie, 2018).

Accordingly, the organizations try to control these forces through marketing policies and new strategies; however, they face uncontrolled forces whether in the home country or foreign countries. For instance, the international marketing business of Nestle, which operates in several foreign countries, may face changes in political stability, economic climate, and class structure that have a direct impact on business decisions and growth. Thus, external forces can create new threats and opportunities in the marketing environment of the company (Ganapavarapu & Chary, 2015). Consequently, the marketers of the company need to understand the context of environmental factors in which marketing operates to use suitable strategies and methods to maintain and develop their ability to serve the customers efficiently and enhance the markets successfully (Jones, 2017).

According to many studies about the most current issues and challenges that impact the international marketing environment of Nestle, they presented three key factors that are discussed below.

2.1.1 Political Condition and Legislation

As Nestle is a multinational company that operates in more than 190 countries, all the political factors can impact its operations or its decisions directly or indirectly as they relate to its international marketing environment in these foreign countries. Actually, political instability exposes its business to risks and threats, as the change in government leads to the creation of new policies and regulations that relate to international business. Such conditions can have a deep impact on the international strategy of Nestle by bringing new threats or opportunities (Jones, 2017). For instance, the Brexit situation created instability in the European Union, which led to the disruption of Nestle's UK food supply chain. So, the company discussed its new plan to replace the production in Newcastle and York with production in Poland as there is no clear vision for the future of the country (Frue, 2019).

Moreover, the political environment involves the laws, regulations, limitations of production, licensing and permits, and taxes that can affect Nestle accordingly. In addition, many countries have implemented investment restrictions, operational restrictions, and discriminatory restrictions. These factors create many current issues in the international market environment, such as supply chain disruption, distribution channel difficulties, and the resulting impact on costs and prices. Therefore, all the marketing activities of Nestle are subject to the legislation of different foreign countries (Frue, 2019). Nestle suffers from the tax costs that are paid to all the countries they operate in, which can decrease its efficiency in marketing as a tax reduces the total amount of consumer and producer surplus. For example, in 2020, Nestle paid around CHF 13.9 billion in incurred (tax borne) and collected taxes from clients, suppliers, and shareholders to the governments in its largest markets, which represent closely the total of the Group's net sales (Nestle, 2020) as shown in Table 3.

Country	Taxes borne	Taxes collected	Total Tax Contribution
Switzerland	1.1	2.9	4.0
USA	1.2	1.0	2.2
France	0.5	0.4	0.9
Brazil	0.2	0.5	0.7
China	0.3	0.3	0.6
Philippines	0.3	0.1	0.4
Germany	0.2	0.1	0.3
India	0.1	0.2	0.3
Italy	0.1	0.2	0.3
Canada	0.1	0.1	0.2
Others	2.1	1.9	4.0
Total	6.2	7.7	13.9

Table 3: The Taxes Borne and Collected by Nestle for the Largest Countries in 2020
Source: (Nestle, 2020)

2.1.2 Economic Forces

The second current issue that Nestle faces is the economic condition of the various countries where it operates. Many countries suffer from low economic growth, eliminating the ability of customers to buy the imported product as the purchasing power of the country is limited. Therefore, the costs that the company incurs when moving its business and production to these countries will not be covered if people cannot buy the products (Maverick, 2021). The economic condition of any country is determined by the stage of development of the economy, the level, the nature of the economy, economic resources, and income distribution, which can all play a significant role in the international market environment.In addition to the other factors such as inflation, currency exchange rates, shipping, productivity, and unemployment, these can have an extremely negative impact on incomes and prices as well (Markgraf, 2022).

For example, in 2020, the foreign exchange of many countries has decreased against the Swiss franc because of many factors, mostly the COVID-19 crisis. Consequently, the sales of the Nestle Group decreased by 7.9%. Besides the divestures that had a negative impact of 4.6%, as a result, the total reported sales decreased by 8.9% to CHF 84.3 billion compared to the previous year, which was CHF 92.6 billion (Nestlé, 2021).

2.1.3 The Social and Cultural Factors

The social and cultural factors are the third current issue that impacts the international marketing environment of Nestle Group strongly. As there are differences in social conditions, thoughts, beliefs, and material culture all impact consumers' perceptions and patterns of buying behavior and attitudes (Agwu & Onwuegbuzie, 2018). Therefore, the company needs to make a profound study of the culture of the target community before offering its products to them. As each company markets its product through marketing promotion by communicating product features to the consumers and influencing them to buy, it should make effective communication to send a message according to the receiver's culture, beliefs, languages, and customs. In addition to understanding how customers think and how they are influenced by their environment, constant changes, and media (Abdin, 2008),

For identifying the impact of this issue on the international market environment, Nestle India's Maggi Noodles ("2-minute For identifying the impact of this issue on the international market environment, Nestle India's Maggi Noodles ("2-minute noodles") will be taken as an example in case the company ignores the impact of culture and crisis communication that forced the company to pay a heavy price for its reputation and its bottom line as well (Dhanesh & Sriramesh, 2018). The story of Maggi instant noodles started as a new product for the Indian market in 1983. It has revolutionized the way Indian people eat breakfast, from evening snacks to morning breakfast, from the south to the north, from dosa to dhokla. It became the leading brand of instant noodles, enjoying a market share of 79.3% in India and the biggest brand portfolio (Podile et al., 2021).

This beloved brand has achieved a long history of success, until the summer of 2015. At that time, everything changed when the Food Safety and Standards Authority of India (FSSAI) found higher lead concentrations than permissible in the noodles. They said each package of noodles contained seven times the permissible level of lead. Therefore, it was banned as unsafe and hazardous for consumption. In response to this campaign, the company worked to control it. But it failed to communicate effectively with consumers as it depended more on its traditional business culture than on its ability to adapt to the changing demands of its environment, which led to the amplification of an issue into a crisis. Customers perceived the brand's complacency and silence as admissions of guilt. In competition, media houses activated aggressive coverage to the point of virality, greatly hindering brand image. The consumers became angry, and the brand crashed faster than any brand to date. As a result, the company announced its first quarterly loss in three decades of Maggi's market share, which dropped from an impressive 80% to below 5% in just a month (Kumari, 2021).

The case of Nestle India's Maggi Noodles crisis shows that many multinational companies face issues that translate into crises. Even though they work hard to control their environment, they face difficulties doing so because they have little control over socio-cultural factors. Nestle struggled over two decades to align itself with the complexities of the cultures in India and achieved success in its business. But it didn't pay much attention to the impact of cultures as environments for crisis communication with its customers, despite their significance. To highlight the cultural impact on crisis communication, it could help overcome the crisis and manage the reputational threat of the foreign organizations (Dhanesh & Sriramesh, 2018).

Chapter 3: Background Analysis

3.1 Marketing Approaches of Nestle in the Local, National, and Regional Marketplace

Nestle has a strong brand because it embraces innovation and provides consumers with the products they want.Nestle operates in 191 countries with 2000 brands to easily provide the needed products through building factories and using the resources of these countries as well. The company offers its products as if it were a local or national company, such as its subsidiaries in India and Nigeria (Markovic, 2018). The company also uses different marketing in different countries to make distribution decisions and pricing decisions and then satisfy different customers' needs and preferences in local and national environments, which made it a multinational company with a famous brand in the world. For example, in 2011, Nestle used the ABC channel to launch the Kit Kat brand through broadcast advertisements recorded in Australian environments to contribute to the sense of national identity (Corona, 2014).

Moreover, the company builds its position in the market through its ingenuity and increased localization approach to match consumer preference in local and national markets. Nestle uses both approaches by encouraging national operations to adapt products locally, respect the local consumers, and give much consideration to their cultural and religious backgrounds, language, regional and national habits and tastes. This helps the company to perceive the local flavors in products and embrace local language by using local names when marketing, and at the same time, helps the company through acquisitions and mergers as the acquired organization has a greater knowledge of local cultures and needs. The company also depends on the local operating managers and gives them the freedom to develop marketing strategies that match local needs through a decentralized approach to management (Markovic, 2018).

For example, Nestlé Nigeria Plc has been operating in Nigeria since 1961, one year after Nigerian independence, when it started the Nestlé operations in Nigeria as a locally based subsidiary of Nestlé. According to the needs of the Nigerian market, the company provided domestic products and chocolate products like Milo, which is the favorite of every child because it contains good vitamins. However, Nestlé operates in Nigeria and across Africa but does not approach the market with the same products and tastes (Bishopton, 2018).

Furthermore, the company adopted a regional cluster-based approach for increasing the growth and penetration of its product. For instance, Nestle India works to adopt this approach to develop a tailor-made brand, distribution strategies, and marketing to address the needs of consumers in specific geographies (Business Line News, 2018).

3.2 International Entry Methods of Nestle SA and its Benefits

Many multinational companies, such as Nestle SA, face many difficulties when trying to expand into foreign markets. It is not easy to choose the international entry methods for new markets as they may expose the company to big risks. Therefore, the international market managers should analyze various strategies at their disposal before making the decision to enter a new market to decrease all the expected risks, ensure successful market entry, and ensure acceptability by the local market regulators. There are two familiar ways that are used by many companies like Nestle: exporting their products to a foreign market or transferring their resources like capital, technology, and operations tools to operate and market their businesses in a new foreign country (Munyiri, 2014).

However, although Nestle SA faced many difficulties in marketing in many foreign countries, it has succeeded in expanding its business in more than 190 countries, and its various products have reached most of the countries around the world. The company depends on a low-cost entry strategy into target markets, such as when it entered the Indian market in 1959, when the company was incorporated and promoted by Nestle Alimentana. The drivers of the international market entry of the company include secure key suppliers, low product costs, and skill deployment. While the international entry methods of the company include alliances, joint ventures, exports, and wholly owned subsidiaries (Greer, 2018), As Nestle is a big multinational company, it is good to keep up its expansion in the world through international entry methods that include joint ventures, foreign direct investment, and wholly-owned subsidiaries, as they will be evaluated along with the three indicators that include the targeted market segment, forecasted market share, and mergers and acquisitions.

3.2.1 Joint Ventures Method

The joint venture marketing method can expand the international marketing of Nestle around the world effectively. The company has used this method with many companies, like Coca-Cola. This entry mode means making an agreement between two companies to integrate marketing strategies that work as a big company to increase market shares, competition, and revenues as well. This method helps the companies increase their advertising audience, transfer the marketing messages to a large number of customers, and crack the toughest markets. Moreover, it can decrease the risks while enhancing the control of the local market by the foreign company. Furthermore, it can help the company access a larger geographical market or a new consumer demographic with its strong brand by launching a new product segment or delivering a new service (Anderson, 2022).

3.2.2 Wholly Owned Subsidiary Method

The wholly owned subsidiary method is used when a companys stock is entirely owned by another company, called the parent company, while the company becomes wholly owned as the result of an acquisition. This method can help Nestle establish its business in foreign countries, as having a wholly owned subsidiary can allow the parent company to have full control over operations, products, and processes in different geographic areas and markets, or in separate sectors. Therefore, these factors can help Nestle deal with changes in the market or geopolitical and trade practices in foreign countries. Accordingly, Nestle SA can increase its market share and produce the new needed segments in various foreign markets according to their demands (Kenton, 2020). Nestle Group has successfully acquired many other companies, including confection companies and successful food companies. For example, in 2001, Nestle acquired Ralston Purina for $10.3 billion, which is an American conglomerate with substantial holdings in animal feed, food, consumer products, pet food, and entertainment (Nestlé, 2001).

3.2.3 Foreign Direct Investment Method

Foreign Direct Investment (FDI) is an internationalization strategy that can help Nestle SA establish a physical presence in foreign countries through the acquisition of productive assets such as technology, capital, labor, plants, land, and equipment. Therefore, the company can expand its operations to new foreign locations and regions. Through this method, Nestle S.A. can enhance its international markets in foreign countries. The company can buy part of or all of an interest in a local company or build its own manufacturing facilities. This can offer advantages that include foreign government investment incentives, secure cost economies in the form of cheaper labor or raw materials, and freight savings. The company can also increase its market share and gain new loyalty from new customers. In addition to creating a good image in the host countries, it creates new jobs. Moreover, the Nestle SA company can build strong relationships with the customers, government, local suppliers, and distributors by offering its favorite products to the local environment. Furthermore, the company can develop innovative manufacturing and marketing policies that serve its long-term international goals (Munyiri, 2014).

3.3. The Impact of the Changing Marketing Business Environment on Nestle SA Company

However, while Nestle SA has successfully expanded its international marketing into new markets around the world, it faces challenges that affect its business due to the change in the business environment. The changing marketing environment can have a profound impact on Nestles marketing priorities and marketing management functions. Any change that occurs in the marketing environment brings threats and opportunities for the company. Therefore, the impact of the changing marketing business environment on Nestle Company would be evaluated through an analysis of the two types of environmental change that include micro forces and macro forces that can create many challenges and issues for the overall strategy and decisions that relate to implementing the marketing activities efficiently and effectively.

3.3.1 Micro Environmental Forces

3.3.1.1 The Supplier

The supplier can have an in-depth impact on the marketing activities of the company. For example, Nestle SA has about 165,000 direct suppliers and about 695,000 individual farmers who provide services, equipment, and raw materials such as milk, seeds, and coffee (Nestlé, 2021). The impact of the supplier determines the efficiency and quality of the company in terms of manufacturing the products, whether negatively or positively. Therefore, in cases of shortage, delays, bad quality, and increased costs of supplies due to natural disasters or other events, these can decrease sales of the company in the short term and lead to customer dissatisfaction in the long term (Philip, 2019).

3.3.1.2 The Customers

The most important player in marketing is the customer, as the company works to gain his loyalty and increase its sales. The types of customers include business markets, government markets, reseller markets, consumer markets, and international markets (Philipp, 2019). For instance, there were rapidly changing consumer preferences and behaviors in 2020, which impacted the sales of many companies around the world, such as Nestle, due to the pandemic (Nestlé, 2021).

3.3.1.3 Marketing Intermediaries

The marketing intermediaries can affect the activity of marketing whether positively or negatively, as they help the company to sell, advertise, distribute, and deliver its product to the end customers on time and safely. They also help the company promote the products to the customers and get feedback from them to take into account. Therefore, Nestle SA works smoothly with all its marketing intermediaries to help provide the best and purest food products to its valuable customers around the world (Ahmed, 2020).

3.3.2 Macro Environmental Forces

3.3.2.1 Economic Forces

Economic factors impact the manufacturing activities of Nestle because of the differences in economic conditions among many countries. The economic condition includes many forces such as inflation, currency exchange rates, shipping, productivity, and unemployment, all of which can have an extremely negative impact on incomes and prices. For example, many countries suffer from low economic growth, which eliminates the ability of customers to buy the imported product as the purchasing power of the country is limited. Therefore, the costs that the company incurs when moving its business and production to these countries will not be covered if people cannot buy the products (Maverick, 2021).

3.3.2.2 Political and Legal Forces:

As discussed in Chapter 2, Nestle SA operates in more than 190 countries, and political and legal forces impact its international marketing activities. As the political environment involves laws, regulations, limitations of production, licensing and permits, and taxes, Nestle SA faces various daily challenges that are related to these factors. Moreover, many governments have imposed investment restrictions, operational restrictions, and discriminatory restrictions. These factors create many current issues in the international market environment, such as supply chain disruption, distribution channel difficulties, and the resulting impact on costs and prices. For example, the Brexit situation created instability in the European Union with new regulations and laws, which led to disrupting the UK food supply chain of the Nestle Company. Such a condition forces the company to rethink its business decisions in this country (Shamsul, 2021).

3.3.2.3 Socio-Cultural Forces

As there are differences in social conditions, thoughts, beliefs, and material culture all impact consumers' perceptions and patterns of buying behavior and attitudes (Agwu & Onwuegbuzie, 2018). Therefore, the company needs to make a profound study of the culture of the target community before offering its products to them. As each company markets its product through marketing promotion by communicating product features to the consumers and influencing them to buy, it should make effective communication to send a message according to the receiver's culture, beliefs, languages, and customs. In addition to understanding how customers think and how they are influenced by their environment, constant changes, and media, we also discussed how these factors could affect Nestle in Chapter 2 (Abdin, 2008).

3.3.2.4 Technological Forces

If the companies fail to update and apply advanced technological changes, they will have difficulty surviving in today's competitive environment. Therefore, technology can create new opportunities for marketers to gain a large market share. Even though Nestle SA has adopted advanced technologies in order to deliver fresher, healthier, and more variety, some countries don't have such advanced technologies for its operations to match the lifestyle of customers, which forces it to import that technology from abroad, which costs it much money (Shamsul, 2021).

Chapter 4: Application of Learning to Practice

4.1 Marketing Strategies

4.1.1 Overview of How to Select an International Market and Develop the Right Entry Strategy

There are many marketing theories and principles that play a great role in choosing an international market and developing an entry strategy for the companies in that market. As discussed above, for entering foreign markets, the company needs strategic decisions that will shape its succeeding activities and its growth opportunities in international markets by using the most suitable market entry modes according to the environmental conditions and competitive situation of the various markets that interest it. It has been shown that Nestle has been dependent on the wholly owned subsidiary method and the foreign direct investment method for entering different foreign markets around the world.

Therefore, the company has to evaluate its basic entry strategy before entering a new country and make choices based on the long-run profitability of different foreign markets. The strategy of the company includes balancing cost, innovation, benefits, and excellence (Nestlé, 2021). While executing the strategies for market development, we need further flexibility, the ability to adapt to unexpected market conditions, and the vision to achieve long-term objectives. Consequently, the company requires the use of suitable marketing strategy tools for evaluating and developing an entry strategy for the organization in an international market.

4.1.2 Evaluation of the Most Suitable Models for Selecting the International Market Entry Methods

According to many studies, the most appropriate marketing tools are to apply both Porter's five forces framework and the Ansoff matrix at the same time. While the Porter model is used for analyzing the external competitive environment of the intended international market to achieve competitive strategy, the Ansoff matrix is used principally for the objective of expanding and growing in the international market (Ward & Rivani, 2014).

4.1.2.1 Compare & Contrast Between the Porter Model and Ansoff Matrix

In this section, it will be discussed how to use the Porter Model and Ansoff Matrix at the same time to design and develop an appropriate strategy for entering the international market by comparing them according to the most important indicators of a successful business, as shown in Table 4.

Thesis Statement:	Applying Porter Model and Ansoff Matrix together as the most appropriate models for selecting the international market entry and develop the strategy of entry in Nestle SA company as well.		
Components	Porter Model	Ansoff Matrix	Analysis
Why these models? Generally, most of the companies looks for entering to new markets for profitability.	This model can help the company evaluate the external market environment and determine its competitiveness before taking the decision to enter new markets to drive competition and profitability (Raihan & Azeem, 2011).	It is a tool for expanding and increasing profits by assessing the level of risk to make the right decision about entering new markets through existing or new products in existing or new markets (Evangelia, 2017).	It figures out that it is good to use both models at the same time for entering a new market. While using Porter's Model to assess the external environment, it uses the Ansoff Matrix to prepare for making the decision to enter a market.
Market Share	It helps the company determine its market share among its competitors. To analyze the change in market share rate and	The best model for increasing market share to match the global competition includes market	As Porter's Model helps determine the market share of the company, the Ansoff

		penetration, diversification, and development factors (Evangelia, 2017).	Matrix helps increase the market share..
	determine the competitive intensity as well (Raihan & Azeem, 2011).		
Marketing Entry Timing	When evaluating the current external factors that can impact the position of the company in the coming year (Raihan & Azeem, 2011).	This model can be used when the company discovers new opportunities to develop a strategy for entering a new market and to be ready to respond to any challenges that may occur (Evangelia, 2017).	While Porter's model identifies the expected factors that can impact the company in the future, the other model helps to make a suitable response.
Entry Market Risk	It has different levels of risk. A high-risk growth strategy occurs when it includes the development of new products or markets (Raihan & Azeem, 2011).	Protect from various risks and uncertainties associated with the strategic marketing plan (Clarissia, 2019)	As Porter's Model figures out the different levels of risk, the Ansoff Matrix produces a strategic marketing plan to face the expected risks..
Prices	It can control the product price in a specific market compared to existing competitors in that market (Raihan & Azeem, 2011).	It can decrease prices to attract new customers · while increasing promotion and distribution efforts (Evangelia, 2017).	While the Porter model can control prices, the Ansoff matrix helps decrease them.

Thesis Conclusion	*According to the previous analysis of the roles of the Porter Model and Ansoff Matrix in forming and developing an international market entry strategy, it was concluded that it was good to use the Porter Model and Ansoff Matrix together. The first step is to use the Porter Model to analyze and discover the environmental circumstances, while the second step is to make the right decision of how to enter the market through forming an effective entry strategy to increase the competitiveness and profitability of Nestle Group as well..*

Table 4 : Compare & Contrast Between the Porter Model and Ansoff Matrix

4.1.3 Analyzing Entry Market Criteria Strategies

4.1.3.1 Porter's Five Forces Model Analysis of Nestle SA Company

As discussed above, Porter's Five Forces is the best model for identifying and examining the external environment of the company and determining its weaknesses and strengths to figure out the level of competition of the company among its competitors through analyzing five competitive forces as detailed in Figure 8.

Figure 8: Porter's Five Forces Model, Source: (Bruin, 2016)

Then, it would evaluate the external market environment and determine the competitiveness of Nestle as the first step to driving competition and profitability before making the decision to enter new markets, as shown in the following (Table 5).

Porter's Five Forces of Nestle Company		
Forces	Scores	Indicators
Threat of New Entrants	Medium	• It can take advantage of high economies of scale. • It has a high marketing budget. • It has a large distribution channel. • It is difficult for a new entrant to compete
Threat of Substitute	High	• It has a large diversified portfolio. • As it has daily use products, it is easy to for the competitors to present substitutes. • It needs to keep producing innovative products to keep attracting customers.
Bargaining Power of Suppliers	Low	• It has a strong relationship with its suppliers. • Farmers are required to maintain high standards. • provides helpful guidance to its suppliers. • Suppliers have a lower power as the company can replace them easily.
Bargaining Power of Buyers	High	• It has a large base of customers globally. • Customers have strong bargaining power as they can find substitutes for products . • There are various similar products offered by the rivals. • It faces enormous competition in the matter of taste, packaging and distribution.
Competitive Rivalry	High	• It has a strong brand that contains 2000 brands.

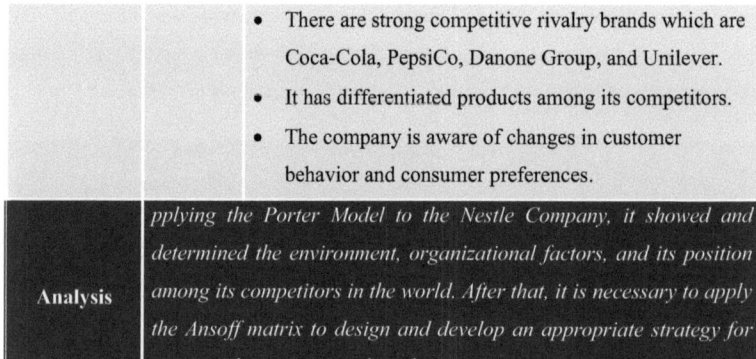

	• There are strong competitive rivalry brands which are Coca-Cola, PepsiCo, Danone Group, and Unilever. • It has differentiated products among its competitors. • The company is aware of changes in customer behavior and consumer preferences.
Analysis	*pplying the Porter Model to the Nestle Company, it showed and determined the environment, organizational factors, and its position among its competitors in the world. After that, it is necessary to apply the Ansoff matrix to design and develop an appropriate strategy for entering the international market.*

Table 5: Porter's Five Forces Model Analysis for Nestle SA Company
Source: (Varma & Ravi, 2017) & (Markovic, 2020)

4.1.3.2. The Ansoff Matrix Analysis of Nestle S.A. Company

After applying the Porter model, it needs to move on to the second step of applying the Ansoff matrix tool, which is used to determine the different strategic options available to the Nestle company to expand its business in the future and enter new markets, whether regionally or internationally. This model helps the company develop entry market strategies, protects it from various levels of risk, and figures out the opportunities available in both new and existing markets through the use of four growth alternatives strategies (Clarissia, 2019), as illustrated in Figure 9 and applied in Table 6.

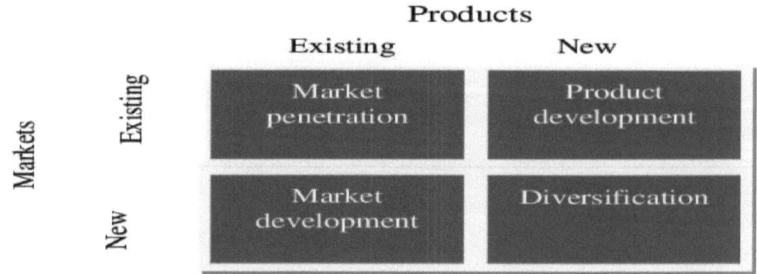

Figure 9: Ansoff Matrix, Source: (Nedelea, 2013)

The Ansoff Matrix Analysis of Nestle SA Company		
	Markets	
	Existing	**New**
Products — **Existing**	*Market Penetration Strategy* ▪ Nestle can have higher penetration through the acquisitions of its competitors and develop leverage through its diversified supply chain and distribution channels to reach different customer groups and segments in existing markets. ▪ The company can enter the market through joint ventures and partnerships with other players in the market to reach large consumer groups while also understanding their market behavior and consumption patterns.	*Market Development Strategy* ▪ The company can expand regionally and take into account any cultural differences to make marketing or product modifications and consumption methods accordingly. ▪ Nestle can enhance its international expansion to increase its market share with new products such as pies and healthy food products.
Products — **New**	*Product Development Strategy* ▪ The company needs to keep investing in research and development to identify market trends and consumer behavior. ▪ After that, the company started to use the NPD process to develop and launch new products in the market for consumers to penetrate new consumer segments, new markets, and target new consumer groups.	*Diversification Strategy* ▪ The company can discover conglomerate growth by entering new markets through mergers and acquisitions and diversifying in these markets that have new consumer groups by offering new products and services.
Analysis & Result	The result of this analysis showed that, Nestle can enter new markets regionally and internationally by depending on three methods: acquisition and merger, joint ventures, and partnerships with other competing market players.	

Table 6: The Ansoff Matrix Analysis of Nestle SA Company, Source: (Harvey, 2020)

4.2 Brand Management

4.2.1 Keller's Brand Equity Model

The most famous theory in brand equity is Keller's Brand Equity Model, also called the Based Brand Equity (CBBE) model, which was made by Kevin Keller in 1993 and developed in 2001 and 2003. He defined it as a model that occurs when the brand becomes known, and the consumer is satisfied with that brand as a favorable, strong, and unique brand. This model identifies four steps for building a strong brand through answering the questions of the customers and contains six brand building blocks (Kuhn & Alpert, 2004), as illustrated in Figure 10.

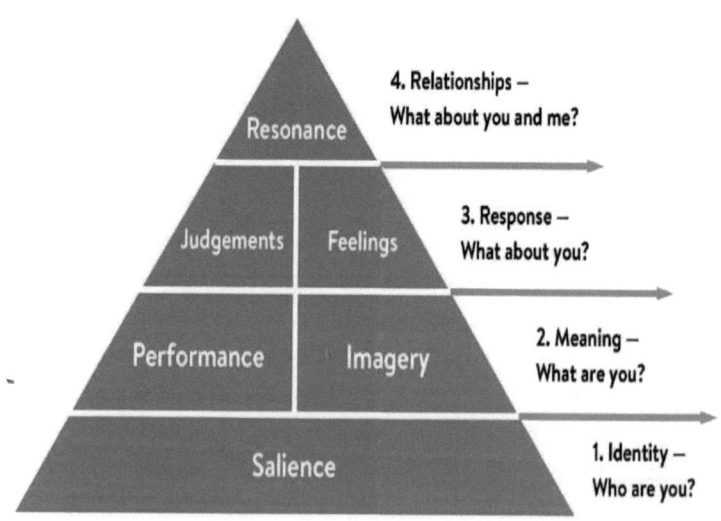

Figure 10: Keller's Customer-Based Brand Equity Pyramid
Source: (Hawker, 2019)

Accordingly, the first stage relates to brand identity and uses brand salience as a measure of the awareness of the brand. This involves linking the logo, the brand name, and the symbol to create a sure association in memory and making sure that customers understand the product or service category in which the brand competes. So, salience has two sub-dimensions that include needing satisfaction and category identification. The second stage focuses on establishing brand meaning by linking tangible and intangible brands, linking either brand performance or image-related associations. The third stage is the brand response, which represents opinions and evaluations of the brand according to the linking of associations identified in judgments that contain overall quality, consideration credibility, and superiority. In addition to the brand's feelings, this refers to the customers' emotional responses and reactions to the brand, which include warmth, excitement, fun, social approval, security, and self-respect. The last stage is brand relationships, where the brand response is transformed to create an intense, active loyalty relationship between customers and the brand through resonance that contains behavioral loyalty, a sense of community, attitudinal attachment, and is active (Kuhn & Alpert, 2004).

4.2.2 The CBBE Model of Nestle Company

When we want to discuss the equity brand of Nestle, it will be discussed about a well-known company that has 2000 brands and can be found everywhere in the world with a strong international competitive market. It can be said that Nestle products can be found in every home around the world, as the company's equity brand offers daily food products that involve cereals, coffee, water, beverages, Nesduik, yoghurt, Opt Fast, performance nutrition, healthcare nutrition, frozen food, refrigerator products, Kit Kat, ice crème, pet food, pet care products, infant food, chocolate, baking food, and eye care heat. The secret to the success of the company is its success in achieving customer satisfaction through the core concept of the brand, which is that good food must be for a good life. Therefore, this success cannot be achieved without having customers' trust, integrity, loyalty, and respect values and without building a long history of strong relationships that make them willing to buy with satisfaction. (Haseeb, 2015).

Therefore, the CBBE model would be applied to the Nestle-Cerelac brand category as it is the most famous baby food around the globe. It was first registered in 1949 as a food for infants from six months on because breast milk alone is not enough for the baby's growing nutritional requirements. The brand has a long history of success as the company uses the steps needed for building a strong brand through the CBBE model, as detailed in Figure 11.

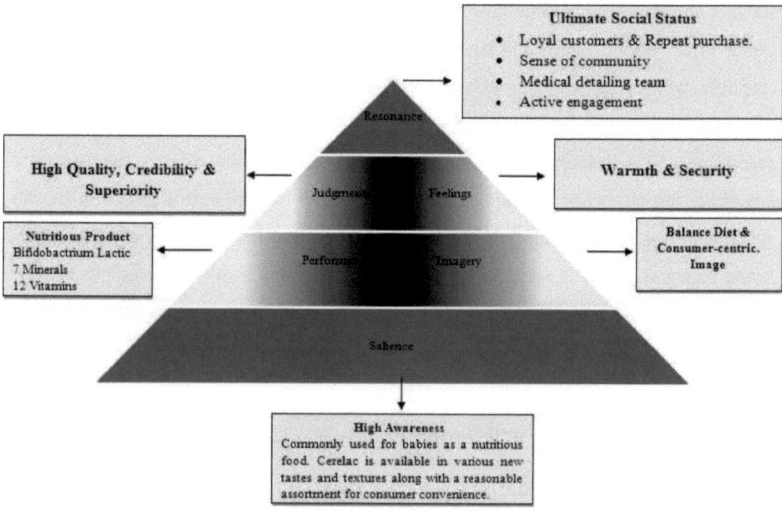

Figure 11: Nestle Cerelac Product Customer-Based Brand Equity Pyramid
Source: (Faheem, 2010)

> ### *The First Level: Salience*

This stage refers to customer awareness of the product. Accordingly, the Cerelac segment has high brand awareness among its customers around the world, as it is commonly used for babies as a nutritious food. It offers various new tastes and textures along with a reasonable mixture of 350 g, 175 g, and 25 g sachet packs to match the customers' desires and needs (Faheem, 2010).

> ### *The Second Level: Performance & Imagery*

Nestle Cerelac becomes very necessary for the babies along with the milk as it contains Bifidobacterium lactic for improving the digestive immunity of their upset tummies. It is present in breast milk as a kind of positive bacteria, and it kills the harmful negative bacteria. In addition, it contains minerals and 12 vitamins, which are necessary for healthier babies. While the imagery of Nestle Cerelac is of a complete balanced diet for healthier, energetic, and active babies among its customers due to its fitting ratio of vitamins, minerals, calcium, and iron in the food, So, the mothers feel free and relaxed about their child's diet needs (Faheem, 2010).

> ### *The Third Level: Judgments & Feelings*

The customers of Nestle's Cerelac product believe in its high quality and believe it is the best choice on the market for their babies. They also judge it to be an innovative and reliable product. Because this product is a pioneer brand and market leader, they feel the brand's superiority in the market, which gives them a sense of calmness, peacefulness, security, and comfort in meeting their needs (Faheem, 2010).

> ### *The Last Level: Resonance*

Resonance level refers to the primary social status of the brand and how much loyalty the customers have for it. This segment has about 40% loyal customers and about 65% repeat customers. There is an active loyalty relationship between customers and the brand as the society is accepting this product and the company has a medical detailing team for mothers consisting of 18,000 doctors belonging to the whole country (Faheem, 2010).

4.2.3 Psychological and Sociological Factors Influencing Consumer Decision Making

Consumers always make the decision of buying products and services according to many factors, most of which are related to the psychological and sociological influences that determine whether they like or dislike the products. Consumers primarily base their buying decisions on the psychological factors that relate to their motivation, learning, socialization, attitudes, and beliefs, in addition to the social factors that relate to their reference groups, social class, and family. Therefore, it would be discussed below the most four impacted factors, which include motivation, learning, family, and reference group (Rangaiah, 2021).

4.2.3.1 Motivation

Consumers have a different level of motivation that affects their buying behavior and marketing decisions. And the basic needs include the psychological needs that include water, food, and sleep. The most famous theory of motivation is made by Maslow through the hierarchy of basic needs that start with psychological needs and move on to safety needs, social needs, esteem needs, and finally self-actualization needs (Rangaiah, 2021), as shown in Figure 12.

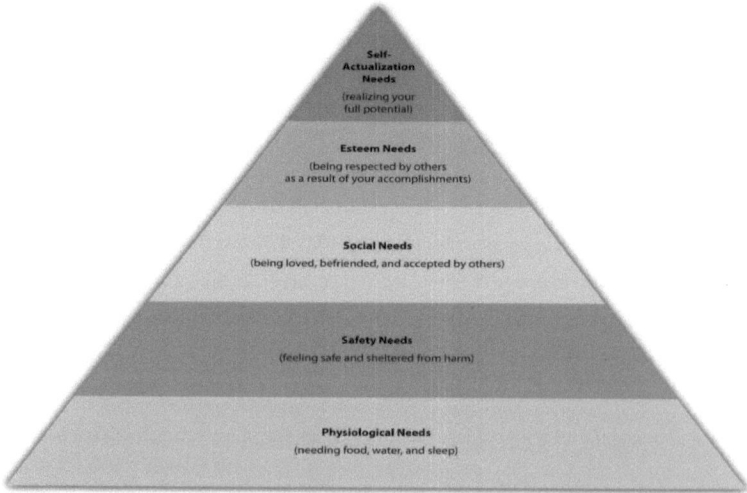

Figure 12: Maslow's Hierarchy of Needs, Source: (Mariadoss, 2017)

4.2.3.2 Learning

Consumers change their decisions and behaviors after gaining information about a product by reading about it, asking questions about it, or having firsthand experience with it. Moreover, the process of learning includes conditional learning or cognitive learning. While conditional learning occurs when the consumers derive learning from being exposed to particular stimuli again and again to get a particular response, Cognitive learning occurs when the consumer uses his knowledge, attitudes, skills, values, and beliefs to make the appropriate purchasing decision for finding satisfaction and fulfilling his needs (Rangaiah, 2021).

3.2.3.3 Family

Every person in the world is influenced by his family, and according to what he has learned from them, he makes his decisions. Therefore, families are considered an important factor that influences the purchasing behaviors of consumers around them. Most of us buy products from specific brands according to what we learn from our parents to buy (Rangaiah, 2021).

4.2.3.4 Reference Group

The reference group refers to a group of people with whom we live, work, and have other contact. We can find them in workplaces, schools, clubs (professional or playgroups), mosques, churches, and even among acquaintances or a group of friends. Therefore, as consumers respect and contact these people, they often ask them about their opinions before they buy goods and services. For example, when a person wants to buy a smartphone or car, he will decide on the purchase according to the advice of his friends (Mariadoss, 2017).

4.2.4 A New Brand Strategy Development for Nestle Company

In 2020, Nestle launched a new brand in the USA called Life Cuisine that is suitable to feed modern lifestyles well by offering delicious and satisfying meal solutions with high protein instead of unhealthy gluten and more vegetables and ingredients that allow them to eat well (Nestlé USA, 2020). As a result, it will be chosen to analyze and critically discuss how to effectively develop the brand strategy step by step, as detailed in Table 7.

Business Strategy	Delivering delicious and satisfying meal solutions for those who like to eat healthy food. This new brand is focusing on offering four consumer preferences that include a high-protein, low-carb lifestyle, a meatless diet, and being gluten-free. It involves 15 recipes for foods that are made with vegetables, protein, and whole grains to be convenient to feed modern lifestyles.
Identify Target Customer	The target consumers are about two-thirds of Americans, as they say their eating habits have changed during the last 5 years, and 3 in 10 say they are making more healthy food choices than a year ago, according to a Nielsen report last December. Therefore, in recent years, Nestle SA has needed to develop this brand to better respond to changing food consumption trends and position more of its business in faster-growing areas in the USA.
Brand Position	The brand should position itself in response to a change in how people want a meal that is suitable for their definition of wellness without compromising on taste or satisfaction. It needs to focus on delivering delicious recipes with more protein, vegetables, and ingredients that allow them to eat well their way, as a registered dietitian and nutrition communication manager at Nestle USA said.
Messaging Strategy	The brand message strategy should attract the attention of the target audience strongly along with its position, such as this statement: New Life Cuisine features on-demand combinations to feed your day, your way.
Name, Logo and Tagline	It needs to make the logo of this brand attractive by writing the main name of this brand in an attractive way. As this brand involves four categories of food products, each one has a name. Low-carb lifestyle, high-protein lifestyle, meatless lifestyle, and gluten-free lifestyle

	In addition to the tagline that comes to describe each name.
	For example, the statement of the tagline of the Gluten-free Lifestyle category is:
	> GLUTEN-FREE & FLAVOR FULL: Make the day delicious with gluten-free pizza, sandwiches, and pasta.
Content Marketing Strategy	Develop the content marketing strategy by creating high-quality content showing how this brand focuses on delivering modern, healthy products with on-trend ingredients that fit a variety of different tastes and needs. This content is offered via blogs, a billboard, TV channels, videos, social media channels, newsletters, and discussion boards. In addition to experimenting with new digital flavors such as chatbots and IoT technology.
Developing Website	Launch a website for the Life Cuisine brand to make consumers aware of the products and services and to help them understand why they need to choose this product. The website of this brand has launched successfully at https://lifecuisine.com/ and contains the story of this brand, what to do and for whom, as well as offering the products that are under this brand with a logo, message strategy, and tagline.
Building Marketing Toolkit	Building a marketing toolkit that can involve sales sheets for describing core product offerings and making pitch decks It also involves video topics about company overviews and case studies, or "meet the partner" videos.
Implementing, Monitoring, and Adjusting	Implementing the brand strategy according to the plan, step by step, along with the deadlines and the timeline and making suitable adjustments if needed In addition to keeping track of all the activities of implementation to make sure whether the strategy is headed in the right direction or not. It is also to measure the forecasted responses and the changing rate of prospective consumers.

Table 7: Nestle Life Cuisine Brand Strategy Development

Source: (Nestlé USA, 2020) & (Frederiksen, 2022)

4.3 New Product Development (NPD)

In the last few years, Nestle SA has adhered to the new product development process (NPD) to meet the nutritional needs and support a balanced diet of consumers who look for the healthiest foods. However, the company has worked to reduce the sugars and sodium in its products, but it is not enough (Morrison, 2021), so it plans to develop new products to feed modern lifestyles well, such as new Life Cuisine products that offer satisfying meal solutions with high protein instead of unhealthy gluten and more vegetables and ingredients that allow them to eat well. Accordingly, the company also plans to use the NPD process to develop new products for the food segment in the future. For achieving the success of the NPD process, one first needs to understand the most common strengths and weaknesses for achieving the NPD process that are discussed below.

4.3.1   The Strengths of New Food Product Development in Nestle Company

4.3.1.1 Gaining New Competitive Advantage

By offering new innovative food products that help to improve the consumer's health and encourage them to eat well, it benefits Nestle Company to attract many customers and gain their loyalty as they can find what they need for modern lifestyle food better than other competitive companies (Nestlé USA, 2020). Consequently, that can increase the market share of the company, which leads to maximizing the revenue of the company globally among its competitors (Azanedo et al., 2020).

4.3.1.2 Increase the Value

Through the NPD process, the company can make sure to produce healthy foods that contain natural ingredients with a minimum amount of sugar and sodium. It refers to the fact that food recipes and processing identified in the NPD process are key to increasing the economic value of food products. Therefore, that helps the company to increase its value, which can reduce the risk, enhance cash flows, and improve the position of the company, which enhances the acquisition strategies globally as well (Azanedo et al., 2020).

4.3.1.3 Boost Quality Control

The NPD process helps the company provide the best quality food to consumers on a large scale. The food recipes need several actions, for example, the adjustment of processing times and temperatures, color, freshness, hygiene conditions in the manufacturing plant, identification of logistics plans that involve storage, consideration of the features of the food product, and the choice of equipment and its working conditions as well. Therefore, the quality of health products can strongly influence the best choice for consumers in modern lifestyles (Azanedo et al., 2020).

4.3.2 The Weaknesses of New Food Product Development in Nestle Company

However, although the food manufacturing sector has succeeded in using the NPD model for many years, it still faces many challenges that are considered weaknesses of the NPD process.

4.3.2.1 Complex and Risky

The NDP process can be a complex and risky operational activity, especially in the manufacturing food sector, as it requires a focus on food safety through knowledge of the quality and standard storage of raw materials, the development of food recipes, formulation, temperature, specific ingredients, desired taste, and the processes needed to safely manufacture the final food product. Therefore, less change in these activities can cause the new product to fail unexpectedly (Azanedo et al., 2020).

4.3.2.2 Changes in Sourcing of Ingredients

ngredients can be a big issue that can make the NDP process inefficient because of their limited availability at certain times of the year if the company depends on seasonal ingredients. Even if the company depends on having a variety of ingredients from different regions of the world, it can decrease the quality of the product if the company doesn't adopt the advanced technology to solve such issues (Azanedo et al., 2020).

4.3.2.3 Shelf Life Stability

Through applying the NPD process in food manufacture, shelf-life stability can be the most critical issue that needs to be tested for physical, biochemical, and chemical factors that affect food quality directly. Many factors can affect food shelf-life stability, such as water activity and the effects plasticization has on temperature, glass transition, and water content. So, the company needs to make sure of how to make suitable packaging for the products that contain grains, vegetables, fruits, and oilseeds effectively (Azanedo et al., 2020). Thus, if the testing has failed, the expected result will be the failure to offer the new product.

4.3.3 International Marketing Strategy

According to what has been discussed about international marketing and based on other studies, a new international marketing strategy for expanding the business of Nestle in the international marketplace would be developed. Therefore, the company should apply the following recommendations in Table 8 and integrate them into the international marketing strategy to make an effective expansion plan.

Nestle International Marketing Strategy for Expanding its Business	
Market Research	For making a new strategy for the expansion, it needs to do research about the new market opportunities regionally and globally. Along with analyzing the product position, the current situation, and the competitive situation by using tools such as SWOT, PESTLE, and Porter's Model.
Figure out the Requirement Products	Understanding the consumers' needs in various geographical locations to meet their local demand successfully through a localization

	approach to prevent risk and failure of entering the new product into the new markets.
Set a Clear Strategy	Making a clear international marketing strategy that is suitable for adoption in the target area. The strategy should be adapted according to external factors such as culture, religion, beliefs, policies, and currencies.
Work with Local Partners	The company should use its local identity to gain exposure in the local market by working with local partners such as local farmers and distributors. The company depends on using local resources and other technologies. It requires establishing competencies and infrastructure in regional factories.
Hiring Local Talent	The company should hire the best local talent that can help gain first-hand knowledge of the market, local culture, and local language skills.
Check the Price	To research price levels in every area that the company enters to adopt a leading price strategy for this international market strategy of new products successfully, taking into account the cost of transport and freight, packaging, and an agent's commission.
Know-How to Promote in the New Environment	It needs to do additional research on how to promote this new product to the target audience and which mediums they are mostly using to attract their attention to the newly offered products. It can depend on many means, such as social media, online advertising, TV channels, radios, and local newspapers.
The Message of Marketing	The company needs to determine the message strategy of the new product to attract the attention of the target audience.
Build a Website	It needs to build a website for the new product to make the consumers aware of the products and services, understand why they need to choose this product, and receive feedback from the consumers as well.
Write a Plan for the New Strategy	To write the international marketing plan on how to implement this strategy for the launch of a new product that includes timescales for accomplishment and the area of the business responsible for the action.

Table 8: Nestle International Marketing Strategy for Expanding its Business
Source: (Eldan, 2021) & (Alan, 2021)

4.3.4 International Marketing Plan

Based on the international marketing strategy recommendations above for expanding the business of Nestle Company in the international marketplace, an international marketing plan would be devised for launching a new food product at Nestle Company. Through the following international marketing plan (Table 9), it will be shown and discussed the processes of how to launch a new food product at Nestle step by step from the beginning to the end of the product project. The timeline of this plan can be implemented in 21 months, from June 1, 2022, to February 30, 2024, as shown in the following table. In addition to measuring the performance of product launches by establishing meaningful KPIs and making continuous improvements to the product.

INTERNATIONAL MARKETING PLAN FOR LAUNCH NEW FOOD PRODUCT IN NESTLE						
STEPS	Key Players	Tasks	Start Date	End Date	Days	Status
Position the New Product	The Global Marketing Team	Make marketing research to: • Identify the target markets. • Understand why the consumers will select the product. • Identify the local and international competitors. • Use techniques such as positioning maps	01-Jun-2022	31-Aug-2022	90	Upcoming

Create a Customer Profile	Design Research Segment	• Collect information of the individual customers that involve age, gender, location, habits, likes, dislikes and other detail to determine who can benefit from the new product.	01-Oct-2022	30-Oct-2022	30	Upcoming
Make a Product Developme nt Roadmap	Technical & Production Department Product Project Manager	• Create a clear a plan of action that outlines the vision, milestones, resources priorities, and progress of the product launch project from the beginning to the end and how they will be achieved them. • Determine the launch dates.	01-Jan-2023	28-Feb-2023	28	Upcoming
Prepare Marketing Team	Product Project Manager	• Make sure of assigning tasks and responsibilities to each employee. • Make the team more accountable and active.	01-Mar-2023	31-Mar-2023	30	Upcoming
Discuss the Strategy	Product Project Manager	• Discussing with all the team about the goal of the strategy and to allow them to share their opinions in how to launch the new product successfully.	01-Apr-2023	09-Apr-2023	9	Upcoming

Prepare Launch Plan	Marketing Project Manager	• Filter all the collecting ideas from the team. • Create a product launch timeline.	10-Apr-2023	30-Apr-2023	20	Upcoming
Make Beta Test	Marketing Project Manager	• Test the product through using it in a production environment to inspect any defect or issue before releasing it.	1-May-2023	30-Jun-2023	30	Upcoming
Get Feedback from Beta Users and Analyze the Results	Product Project Manager Technical & Production Department	• Collect the feedback from the Beta tester and to analyses it to ensure if the product meets requirements and expectations or not. • Make the final product change according to the received feedback and suggestions.	01-Jul-2023	30-Jul-2023	30	Upcoming
Go-to-Market Strategy	The Product Marketing Manager	• Determine the pricing strategy for competitive advantage. • Choose the appropriate distribution and marketing channels.	01-Aug-2023	15-Aug-2023	15	Upcoming
Identify Promoter/ Affiliates	Global Affiliate Marketing Manager	• Determine the affiliate marketing promotion methods and for launching the new product. regionally and globally.	16-Aug-2023	30-Aug-2023	14	Upcoming

Announce the Launch	Email Marketing Manager	• Sending a marketing message to inform people about an upcoming product that include the name and images, the main benefits, the launch date, and clarifying the value of the product.	01-Oct-2023	30-Oct-2023	30	Upcoming
	Regional Marketing Manager	• Initiate product brochures, sell sheets and data sheets.				
Inviting People to Come to the Big Event	Marketing Product Promoter	• Inviting and Motivating people to come and buy the product by offering incentives such as free shipping and a discount.	01-Nov-2023	30-Nov-2023	30	Upcoming
Website Set-Up and Launch it	Digital Marketing Department	• Make a Website for the new product that contains all the features of the products and launch when it is ready.	01-Dec-2023	30-Dec-2023	30	Upcoming
Start Social Media Announcement	R&D Department	• Make research where the customer's media preferences to make a decision on which media channels should use for announcing the new product.	01-Jan-2024	30-Jan-2024	30	Upcoming
	Global Marketing Manager	• Using effective communication strategy should engage cross-				

		functional and cross-regional team members.				
Do the Big Event	All the Members of Team Digital Marketing Team	• Make a milestone event and maintain entertainment during event. • Launch a social campaign and recognition campaign. • Highlight the event happenings and share it in the online channels.	01-Feb-2024	07-Feb-2024	7	Upcoming
Keep Promoting the Product by Online Tools	Digital Marketing Team	• Making Ads by paid traffic. • Check all the links. • Update all the online channels for promotion such as Website and social media.	08-Feb-2024	30-Feb-2024	22	Upcoming
Follow-Up	The Regional Product Manager	• Keep tracking the performance of the product for the 2 coming years. • Make KPIs for the performance of the product.	01-Mar-2024	NA	NA	Upcoming
Continuous Improveme nt	The Regional Product Manager	• Make an ongoing improvement of product through incremental and breakthrough improvements over time.	01-Mar-2024	NA	NA	Upcoming

9: International Marketing Plan for Launch New Food Product in Nestle

Source: (Athuraliya, 2021

Chapter 5: Recommendations and Conclusion

5.1 Recommendations

Through the previous discussion and analysis in this report of the international marketing management practices of Nestle Company and what and how to select and implement a marketing strategy to expand its business in the global market, it was found that, Nestle still faces many challenges and issues in applying an adequate marketing strategy in the global market for expanding its business. Based on that analysis and evaluation, it figured out the following recommendations to provide sufficient marketing strategies to expand the business in the global market of the Nestle SA company successfully.

❖ Understanding how customers think and how they are influenced by their environment, constant changes, and media The company has to evaluate its basic entry strategy before entering a new country and make choices based on the long-run profitability of different foreign markets.

❖ The market strategy of the company should involve balancing cost, innovation, benefits, and excellence for entering a new market.

❖ Through executing the strategies for market development, the company needs further flexibility, the ability to adapt to unexpected market conditions, and the vision to achieve long-term objectives.

❖ The company needs to make a profound study of the culture of the target community before offering its products to them.

❖ It needs to highlight the cultural impact on crisis communication to overcome the crisis and manage the reputational threat to the company.

❖ The best methods for expanding its market business in new markets, whether regionally or internationally, are foreign direct investment, wholly owned subsidiaries, acquisition and merger, joint ventures, and partnerships with other competing market players.

❖ Expanding ready-to-eat healthy food in the new merger markets to meet the nutritional needs and support a balanced diet of modern consumers who look for the healthiest food.

❖ Develop the content marketing strategy by creating high-quality content showing how this brand focuses on delivering modern, healthy products with on-trend ingredients that fit a variety of different tastes and needs.

❖ applying the Porter Model and Ansoff Matrix together as the most appropriate models for selecting the international market entry and developing the strategy of entry in Nestle SA as well.

5.2 Conclusion

In conclusion, this report has discussed and analyzed the main concepts of marketing management, including its models and techniques, in a practical context and applied them to Nestles marketing strategy. It showed that Nestle is a famous multinational company with its vision and mission of believing that providing good food is the main source of good health throughout life. It showed that Nestle has depended on the localization approach to market its products globally in several geographical locations by understanding local flavors and preferences in products and using local language in marketing as well. The company has a long history of adopting an acquisition strategy to expand and penetrate new international markets.

This study also identified three key international marketing environment challenges for the company, which include the political conditions and instability that create new legislation, the economic condition of the various countries, and social and cultural factors. After that, it suggested how Nestle can keep using international entry methods that include joint ventures, foreign direct investment, and wholly owned subsidiaries.

Moreover, it presented how to apply the Porter Model and Ansoff Matrix together for selecting the international market entry and develop the strategy of entry for Nestle SA as well. Furthermore, it identified brand management through the CBBE model of Nestle Company. In addition to identifying how Nestle can develop its new brand strategy in the USA, which is called the Life Cuisine brand, The report figured out the strengths of the NPD process, which involve increasing the competitive advantage, quality, and value of the company, as well as its weaknesses, including its complexity and risk, changes in the sourcing of ingredients, and shelf-life stability. Finally, it provided an international marketing strategy for expanding Nestle's business with needed recommendations to make an effective expansion plan that was discussed step by step accordingly.

References

1. Abdin, M. J.(2008). Impact of Culture on International Marketing. *SSRN Electronic Journal,* p. DOI:10.2139/SSRN.1267863.

2. Addison, (2019). *Marketing Mix Nestle.* [Online] Available at: https://www.essay48.com/term-paper/13633-Nestle-Marketing-Mix [Accessed 16 March 2022].

3. Agwu, M. E. & Onwuegbuzie, H. N. (2018). Effects of international marketing environments on entrepreneurship development. *Journal of Innovation and Entrepreneurship,* 7(12), pp. 1-14.

4. Ahmed, W. (2020). *Micro And Macro Environment Of Nestle.* [Online] Available at: https://pdfcookie.com/documents/micro-and-macro-environment-of-nestle-z3ld6ry7qg24 [Accessed 17 February 2022].

5. Alan, (2021). *Globalizationpedia: 5 Strategies for Successful International Market Expansion.* [Online] Available at: https://globalizationpedia.com/market-expansion/ [Accessed 09 March 2022].

6. Anderson, C. (2022). *CHRON: What Is Joint Venture Marketing?.* [Online] Available at: https://smallbusiness.chron.com/joint-venture-marketing-30933.html [Accessed 10 February 2022].

7. Athuraliya, A. (2021). *Creately: The Visual Guide to Launching a New Product.* [Online] Available at: https://creately.com/blog/marketing/guide-to-launching-a-product/ [Accessed 12 March 2022].

8. Azanedo, L., Garcia-Garcia , G., Stone, J. & Rahimifard, S. (2020). An overview of current challenges in new food product development. *Sustainability (Switzerland) - MDPI,* 12(8), pp. 10-14.

9. Bishopton, M. I. (2018). Adaptation of Marketing Strategy of Multinational Companies on Foreign Local. *Bachelor's thesis: International Business Administration-TALLINN UNIVERISTY OF TECHNOLOGY.*

10. Bruin, L. D. (2016). *Business-to-you: Porter's Five Forces.* [Online] Available at: https://www.business-to-you.com/porters-five-forces/ [Accessed 23 February 2022].

11. Business Line News, (2018). *Nestle India to adopt regional cluster strategy to boost volume.* [Online] Available at: https://www.thehindubusinessline.com/news/nestle-india-to-adopt-regional-cluster-strategy-to-boost-volume/article22859839.ece [Accessed 3 February 2022].

12. Clarissia, M. S. (2019). A STUDY ON ANSOFF MATRIX TECHNIQUE: AS A GROWTH STRATEGY AND AN ADAPTIVE LEARNING TECHNIQUE ADOPTED IN THE LEADING BRAND OF PRODUCTS. *A JOURNAL OF COMPOSITION THEORY,* XII(IX), pp. 1494-1506.

13. Corona, E. M. (2014). Comparison of Marketing Policies Applied By the Same Company in Different.

14. Dhanesh, G. S. & Sriramesh, K. (2018). Culture and Crisis Communication: Nestle India's Maggi Noodles Case. *Journal of International Management,* 24(3), pp. 204-214.

15. Eldan, U. (2021). *6 Crucial Steps for Creating Your Global Expansion Strategy.* [Online] Available at: https://www.omnipresent.com/resources/how-to-create-a-global-expansion-strategy [Accessed 09 March 2021].

16. Evangelia, T. (2017). Application of Ansoff's Matrix-Methodology:Marketing Growth Strategies For Products Tsatsoula Evangelia. *Thessaloniki,Greece - Master Of Science in Strategic Product Design .*

17. Faheem, (2010). *Nestle Cerelac Customer-Based Brand Equity Pyramid (CBBE).* [Online] Available at: https://www.onlinemarketingicons.com/2010/07/nestle-cerelac-customer-based-brand.html [Accessed 28 Februray 2020].

18. Frederiksen, L. (2022). *Hingemarketing: A 10 Step Brand Development Strategy for Your Professional Services Firm.* [Online] Available at: https://hingemarketing.com/blog/story/a_10_step_brand_development_strategy_f or_your_professional_services_firm [Accessed 5 March 2022].

19. Frue, K. (2019). *PESTLE ANALYSIS: PEST Analysis of Nestle: How politics and social culture affect its growth.* [Online] Available at: https://pestleanalysis.com/pest-analysis-of-

nestle/#:~:text=Political%20factors%3A%20The%20company's%20ability,of%20 governmental%20policies%20and%20changes. [Accessed 28 January 2021].

20. Ganapavarapu, L. K. & Chary, S. R. K. (2015). International Marketing Environment Challenges and Opportunities. *International Journal of Science and Research (IJSR),* 4(8), pp. 1836-1838.

21. Greer, G. (2018). Win in India: An Analysis of Market Entry Strategy Into India's Food and Beverage Industry. *Business Administration in Finance and Accounting,* p. http://scholarworks.uark.edu/finnuht/39.

22. Hanlon, A. (2022). *Smartinsights: The segmentation, targeting, positioning (STP) marketing model.* [Online] Available at: https://www.smartinsights.com/digital-marketing-strategy/customer-segmentation-targeting/segmentation-targeting-and-positioning/#:~:text=The%20STP%20model%20is%20useful,market%20targetin g%2C%20and%20product%20positioning. [Accessed 17 March 2022].

23. Harvey, M. (2020). *Essay48: Ansoff Matrix Of Nestle.* [Online] Available at: https://www.essay48.com/13633-Nestle-Ansoff-Matrix [Accessed 25 February 2022].

24. Haseeb, (2015). *Marketindawn: Brand Equity of Nestle.* [Online] Available at: https://www.marketingdawn.com/brand-equity-of-nestle/ [Accessed 28 February 2022].

25. Hawker, K. (2019). *Medium: Keller's Brand Equity Model — What It Is & How to Use It.* [Online] Available at: https://medium.com/@keatonhawker/kellers-brand-equity-model-what-it-is-how-to-use-it-84e42d562299 [Accessed 27 February 2022].

26. Jones, G. (2017). Harvard Business School. *International Business and Emerging Markets: A Long-Run Perspectiv,* pp. 1-41.

27. Kenton, W. (2020). *Iinvestopedia: Wholly Owned Subsidiary.* [Online] Available at:https://www.investopedia.com/terms/w/whollyownedsubsidiary.asp#:~:text=Ke y%20Takeaways-,A%20wholly%20owned%20subsidiary%20is%20a%20company%20whose%20c ommon%20stock,operations%2C%20products%2C%20and%20processes. [Accessed 13 February 2022].

28. Kuhn, K. & Alpert, F. (2004). Applying Keller's Brand Equity Model in a B2B Context: Limitations and an Empirical Test. *Journal of Marketing Management,* 23(5-6), pp. 483-496.

29. Kumari, G. (2021). *The Strategy Story: Dramatic story of Maggi in India: a lesson in brand management.* [Online] Available at: https://thestrategystory.com/2021/01/07/story-of-maggi-in-india/ [Accessed 31 Janaury 2022].

30. Mariadoss, B. J. (2017) . *opentext: 5.1 Factors That Influence Consumers' Buying Behavior.* [Online] Available at: https://opentext.wsu.edu/marketing/chapter/5-1-factors-that-influence-consumers-buying-behavior/ [Accessed 02 March 2022].

31. Markgraf, B. (2022). *Chron: The Impact of Economics on International Marketing.* [Online] Available at: https://smallbusiness.chron.com/advantage-globalization-trade-opportunities-73571.html [Accessed 29 January 2022].

32. Markovic, M. (2018). Strategic Analysis Report Nestlé S.A.. *University of Roehampton London - Business School,* p. https://www.researchgate.net/publication/328968077_Nestle's_Strategic_Analysis_Report.

33. Markovic, M. (2020). Strategic Analysis Report Nestlé S.A.. *University of Roehampton, Business School .*

34. Maverick, J. (2021). *Investopedia: Which Economic Factors Most Affect the Demand for Consumer Goods?.* [Online] Available at: https://www.investopedia.com/ask/answers/042815/which-economic-factors-most-affect-demand-consumer-goods.asp [Accessed 29 January 2022].

35. Morrison, O. (2021). *Nestlé confirms new health and nutrition strategy after leaked documents dent.* [Online] Available at: https://www.foodbusinessnews.net/articles/18456-nestle-launching-10-new-life-cuisine-offerings#:~:text=The%20new%20Life%20Cuisine%20offerings,%2C%20meatless%20and%20gluten%2Dfree. [Accessed 06 March 2022].

36. Munyiri, M. M. (2014). MARKET ENTRY STRATEGIES USED BY MULTINATIONAL CORPORATIONS TO ENTER INTO KENYAN MARKET. *Department Business Administration School of Business University of Nairobi.*

37. Nedelea, A. (2013). BUSINESS STRATEGIES IN TOURISM. *Journal of Ecoforum,* Volume 2.

38. Nestlé USA, (2020). *Nestlé Introduces New Life Cuisine To Feed Modern Ways Of Eating Well.* [Online] Available at: https://www.nestleusa.com/media/pressreleases/allpressreleases/nestle-introduces-life-cuisine-to-feed-modern-wellness-eating [Accessed 03 March 2022].

39. Nestlé, (2001). *Nestlé and Ralston Purina Announce the Creation of a Major International Pet-Care Business.* [Online] Available at: https://www.nestle.com/media/pressreleases/allpressreleases/purina-16jan01 [Accessed 14 February 2022].

40. Nestle, (2020a). *Nestle: Corporate Business Principles.* [Online] Available at: https://www.nestle.com/sites/default/files/asset-library/documents/library/documents/corporate_governance/corporate-business-principles-en.pdf [Accessed 16 January 2021].

41. Nestle, (2020b). *Nestle: Our Impact - Effective Tax Rate and Tax Payments.* [Online] Available at: https://www.nestle.com/csv/what-is-csv/taxation#:~:text=In%202020%2C%20Nestl%C3%A9%20incurred%20CHF,the%20geographic%20and%20business%20mix, [Accessed 28 January 2022].

42. Nestlé, (2021). *Nestlé: Nestlé Global Annual Review 2020.* [Online] Available at: https://www.nestle.com/sites/default/files/2021-03/2020-annual-review-en.pdf [Accessed 16 January 2021].

43. Philip, B. (2019). *Linkeden: Micro and Macro environment factors to be analyzed for companies.* [Online] Available at: https://www.linkedin.com/pulse/micro-macro-environment-factors-analyzed-companies-bobin-philip/ [Accessed 15 February 2022].

44. Podile, V., Deepa, E. & Saujanya, J. (2021). Importance of Consumer Behavior -A Case Study of Maggi Noodle , Nestle India. *Turkish Online Journal of Qualitative Inquiry (TOJQI),* 12(8), p. 7689 – 7697.

45. Prachi, M. (2019). *The Investors Book: Global Marketing Vs International Marketing.* [Online] Available at: https://theinvestorsbook.com/global-marketing-vs-international-marketing.html [Accessed 21 Januray 2022].

46. Raihan, R. & Azeem, S., 2011. The specificities of market entry strategies into a developing country. *Masters Thesis in Marketing, 4FE02E, 15 hp, Spring 2011 Linnaeus University, Växjö, Sweden.*

47. Rangaiah, M. (2021). *Analyticssteps: 5 Factors Influencing Consumer Behavior.* [Online] Available at: https://www.analyticssteps.com/blogs/5-factors-influencing-consumer-behavior [Accessed 1 March 2022].

48. Reza, M. H. (2020). Analysis of Marketing Strategy and Quality Policy of Nestlé. *International Journal of Scientific Research and Engineering Development,* 3(2), pp. 1145-1152.

49. Shamsul, (2021). *PESTLE ANALYSIS OF NESTLE.* [Online] Available at: https://wiselancer.net/pestle-analysis-of-nestle/ [Accessed 17 February 2022].

50. Singh, P., Jian, O. Z. & Mui, D. (2021). A Study on Nestle Promotion Strategy. *International Journal of Accounting & Finance in Asia Pasific,* Volume 4, pp. 60-70.

51. Topper, (2022). *Topper: Market – Meaning and Classification.* [Online] Available at: https://www.toppr.com/guides/business-economics/meaning-and-types-of-markets/market-meaning-and-classification/ [Accessed 21 January 2022].

52. Varma, G. R. & Ravi, J. (2017). Strategic Analysis on FMCG Goods: A Case Study on Nestle. *International Journal of Research in Management,* 4(12-22), p. 2.

53. Ward, D. & Rivani, E. (2014). An Overview of Strategy Development Models and the Ward-Rivani Model. *European School of Economics, Via Chiaravalle 9, 20100 Milan, Italy.,* pp. 1-24.

54. Yadav, S. (2009). *Business Management Paper III - Marketing Management.* 2 ed. Mumbai : Institute of Distance Education, University of Mumbai.